CROWN CLASSICS

EDWARD LEAR
SELECTED POEMS

Lear showing a doubting stranger his name in his hat to prove that Edward Lear was a man and not merely a name.

Drawn by Himself.

CROWN CLASSICS

Edward Lear

Selected Poems

Selected and introduced by
Louise Guinness

MOUNT ORLEANS
PRESS

Crown Classics Poetry Series
Series editor: Louise Guinness

This collection first published in 2019 by
Mount Orleans Press
23 High Street, Cricklade SN6 6AP
https://anthonyeyre.com

Volume © 2019 Mount Orleans Press
All rights reserved
"Crown Classics" is a registered trade mark

CIP data for this title are available from the British Library

Typography and book production by Anthony Eyre

ISBN 978-1-912945-08-5

Printed in Italy
by Esperia, Lavis (TN)

Frontispiece:
Edward Lear self-portrait with Hat
Wikimedia Commons

CONTENTS

INTRODUCTION

EDWARD LEAR did not have a promising start in life. By his own account he was the twentieth of 21 children born to Jeremiah and Ann Lear in Holloway in North London. In childhood he suffered from asthma and bronchitis and, from the age of six, epilepsy. Throughout his life he was prone to depression, bouts of melancholy he referred to as 'The Morbids'. His mother took very little interest in him but in his eldest sister, Ann, 21 years his senior, he had a loving, nurturing mother-figure. In 1827 when Lear was not yet 15 years old his parents retired to Gravesend. Ann and Edward remained in the city, taking up lodgings near the Gray's Inn Road. Encouraged by Ann, he began to draw 'for bread and cheese' and a few years later in the summer of 1830 he was employed by the Zoological Society as a serious ornithological draughtsman. He embarked on an ambitious project to illustrate a book on a single species of birds and he chose parrots. His *Illustrations of the Family of Psittacidae, or Parrots* was to appear in a large folio size in fourteen numbers funded by subscribers but he had to stop short of the promised fourteen when he ran out of money.

He caught the eye of the immensely rich and benign Earl of Derby who had a private menagerie at Knowsley Hall near Liverpool and from 1832 to 1836 Lord Derby employed Lear to draw precise anatomical drawings of his birds and animals. He also worked for John Gould helping him with illustrations for his *Birds of Europe*. Lear's eyesight was under strain from the close work of ornithological drawing and in the autumn of 1836 he wrote to Gould 'that no bird under an ostrich shall I soon be able to do'. He decided to abandon zoological drawing and turned to topographical landscape. It was in this medium that he made his living for the rest of his life, travelling extensively to Italy, Albania, Illyria, Calabria and Corsica. He also visited and sketched Egypt, the Holy Land, Greece and India. He never lived permanently in England again, but choose instead to live in Italy, first in Rome and then, in his later years, in San Remo on the Italian Riviera.

His nonsense poems describe another landscape altogether and they were always composed as a side line to his professional life. He composed rhymes to amuse Lord Derby's grandchildren at Knowsley and published them his first *Book of Nonsense* in 1845 under a pseudonym – Derry down Derry. He later gathered this work together and added to it and published a second book of nonsense under his own name in 1861. Lear popularised the limerick and the verse form became something of a craze in Victorian England. The longer more melancholy nonsense songs were composed during the 1870s when Lear had settled in San Remo. He had no inkling during his lifetime that these poems, the songs, the nonsense, the 'bosh' as he called it would outshine his landscapes and become his brightest legacy.

G. K. Chesterton once wrote that Lear's poems 'constitute an entirely new discovery in literature, the discovery that incongruity itself may constitute a harmony' and that if 'Lewis Carroll is great in this lyric insanity, Mr Edward Lear is, to our mind, even greater.' It is no accident that nonsense verse really took hold of the public imagination in the Victorian era. A time of such unparalleled earnestness was bound to have a backlash and a delight in absurdity as well

as the signalling of possibilities beyond the realm of con-
formity marks the greatest of Lear's nonsense. Misfits and
outsiders, not human, but always full of humanity, yearn
for freedom from the considerable constraints of society,
away from the disapproval of a stuffy chorus, often 'they'.
The solution is often escape to faraway lands - the Hills of
the Chankley Bore or the Land where the Bong Tree Grows.
The Dong with the Luminous Nose wanders, forlornly, it
must be said, over the Great Gromboolian Plain; sometimes
they are saved by peculiar friendships: the Pobble who has
no toes is comforted by kindly Aunt Jobiska who

> '...made him a feast at his earnest wish
> Of eggs and buttercups fried with fish;—
> And she said,—'it's a fact the whole world knows,
> That Pobbles are happier without their toes.'

And the Quangle Wangle welcomes simply everyone to his
hat:

> And the golden grouse came there,
> And the Pobble who has no toes, -
> And the small Olympian bear,
> And the Dong with the luminous nose,
> And the blue baboon, who played the flute,
> And the orient calf from the land of Tute
> And the Attery Squash and the Bisky Bat
> All came and built on the lovely hat
> Of the Quangle Wangle Quee.

Mismatched couples doggedly ignore their differences and
the incongruity of their outward appearances. The Duck
and the Kangaroo, the Daddy-Long-Legs and the Fly and,
most famously, The Owl and the Pussycat are piercing love
stories. Society may say such a thing is impossible but in
Lear's poetry the power of love trumps the limitations of

convention. Once they have sailed away for a year and a day, the Owl and the Pussycat have one of the sweetest courtships in all of literature. Their wedding feast is simple – mince and slices of quince eaten with a runcible spoon

And hand in hand, on the edge of the sand,
They danced by the light of the moon,
The moon,
The moon,
They danced by the light of the moon.

Edward Lear never married. He was a firmly closeted Victorian gentleman and any evidence of requited passions was destroyed. Incredible as it now seems homosexuality was regarded as a crime and right up until 1861 carried a maximum penalty of death. He had many friends, including Tennyson, whose poems he illustrated and his last years were spent comfortably in his villa in San Remo attended by his servant Giorgio and his tremendous cat, Foss whom he immortalised in a series of heraldic drawings. He died peacefully on 29 January 1888 at the age of 76. His headstone bears an inscription by Tennyson:

– all things fair
with such a pencil such a pen
You shadow'd forth to distant men
I read and felt that I was there.

THE OWL AND THE PUSSY-CAT

THE Owl and the Pussy-Cat went to sea
 In a beautiful pea-green boat,
They took some honey, and plenty of money,
 Wrapped up in a five-pound note.
The Owl looked up to the stars above,
 And sang to a small guitar,
'O Lovely Pussy! O Pussy, my love,
 What a beautiful Pussy you are,
  You are,
  You are!
 What a beautiful Pussy you are!'

Pussy said to the Owl, 'You elegant fowl!
 'How charmingly sweet you sing!
'O let us be married! too long we have tarried
 'But what shall we do for a ring?'
They sailed away for a year and a day,
 To the land where the Bong-tree grows,
And there in a wood a Piggy-wig stood,
 With a ring at the end of his nose,
  His nose,
  His nose,
 With a ring at the end of his nose.

'Dear Pig, are you willing to sell for one shilling
   'Your ring?' Said the Piggy, 'I will.'
So they took it away, and were married next day
   By the Turkey who lives on the hill.
They dined on mince, and slices of quince,
   Which they ate with a runcible spoon;
And hand in hand, on the edge of the sand,
   They danced by the light of the moon,
     The moon,
     The moon,
   They danced by the light of the moon.

THE DUCK AND THE KANGAROO

SAID the Duck to the Kangaroo,
   'Good gracious! how you hop!
Over the fields and the water too,
   As if you never would stop!
My life is a bore in this nasty pond,
And I long to go out in the world beyond!
   I wish I could hop like you!'
   Said the Duck to the Kangaroo.

'Please give me a ride on your back!'
   Said the Duck to the Kangaroo.
'I would sit quite still, and say nothing but
   "Quack,"
The whole of the long day through!
And we'd go to the Dee, and the Jelly Bo Lee,
Over the land, and over the sea;—
   Please take me a ride! O do!'
   Said the Duck to the Kangaroo.

Said the Kangaroo to the Duck,
   'This requires some little reflection;
Perhaps on the whole it might bring me luck,
   And there seems but one objection,
Which is, if you'll let me speak so bold,
You feet are unpleasantly wet and cold,
   And would probably give me the roo-
   Matiz!' said the Kangaroo.

Said the Duck, 'As I sat on the rocks,
   I have thought over that completely,
And I bought four pairs of worsted socks
   Which fit my web-feet neatly.
And to keep out the cold I've bought a cloak.
And every day a cigar I'll smoke,
   All to follow my own dear true
   Love of a Kangaroo!'

Said the Kangaroo, 'I'm ready!
   All in the moonlight pale;
But to balance me well, dear Duck, sit steady!
   And quite at the end of my tail!'
So away they went with a hop and a bound,
And they hopped the whole world three times
     round;
   And who so happy,—O who,
   As the Duck and the Kangaroo?

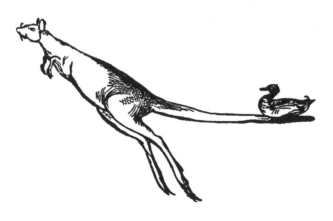

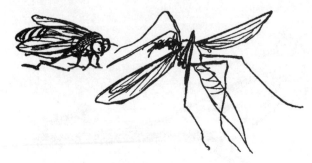

THE DADDY LONG-LEGS AND THE FLY

ONCE Mr Daddy Long-Legs,
   Dressed in brown and gray,
Walked about upon the sands
   Upon a summer's day;
And there among the pebbles,
   When the wind was rather cold,
He met with Mr Floppy Fly,
   All dressed in blue and gold.
And as it was too soon to dine,
They drank some Periwinkle-wine,
And played an hour, two or more,
At battlecock and shuttledore.

Said Mr Daddy Long-Legs
   To Mr Floppy Fly,
'Why do you never come to court?
   I wish you'd tell me why.
All gold and shine, in dress so fine,
   You'd quite delight the court.
Why do you never go at all?

I really think you *ought*!
And if you went, you'd see such sights!
Such rugs! and jugs! and candlelights!
And more than all, the King and Queen,
One in red, and one in green!'

'O Mr Daddy Long-Legs,'
　　Said Mr Floppy Fly,
'It's true I never go to court,
　　And I will tell you why.
If I had six long legs like yours,
　　At once I'd go to court!
But oh! I can't, because *my* legs
　　Are so extremely short.
And I'm afraid the King and Queen
(One in red, and one in green)
Would say aloud, "You are not fit,
You Fly, to come to court a bit!"'

'O Mr Daddy Long-Legs,'
　　Said Mr Floppy Fly,
'I wish you'd sing one little song!
　　One mumbian melody!
You used to sing so awful well
　　In former days gone by,
But now you never sing at all;
　　I wish you'd tell me why:
For if you would, the silvery sound
Would please the shrimps and cockles round,
And all the crabs would gladly come
To hear you sing, "Ah, Hum di Hum!"'

Said Mr Daddy Long-Legs,
　　'I can never sing again!
And if you wish, I'll tell you why,
　　Although it gives me pain.

For years I could not hum a bit,
    Or sing the smallest song;
And this the dreadful reason is,
    My legs are grown too long!
My six long legs; all here and there,
Oppress my bosom with despair;
And if I stand, or lie, or sit,
I cannot sing one single bit!'

So Mr Daddy Long-Legs
    And Mr Floppy Fly
Sat down in silence by the sea,
    And gazed upon the sky.
They said, 'This is a dreadful thing!
    The world has all gone wrong,
Since one has legs too short by half,
    The other much too long!
One never more can go to court,
Because his legs have grown too short;
The other cannot sing a song,
Because his legs have grown too long!'

Then Mr Daddy Long-Legs
    And Mr Floppy Fly
Rushed downward to the foaming sea
    With one sponge-taneous cry;
And there they found a little boat
    Whose sails were pink and gray;
And off they sailed among the waves
    Far, and far away.
They sailed across the silent main
And reached the great Gromboolian plain;
And there they play for evermore
At battlecock and shuttledore.

THE JUMBLIES

THEY went to sea in a Sieve, they did,
　　In a Sieve they went to sea:
In spite of all their friends could say,
On a winter's morn, on a stormy day,
　　In a Sieve they went to sea!
And when the Sieve turned round and round,
And every one cried, 'You'll all be drowned!'
They called aloud, 'Our Sieve ain't big,
But we don't care a button! we don't care a fig!
　　In a Sieve we'll go to sea!'
　　　　Far and few, far and few,
　　　　　　Are the lands where the Jumblies live;
　　　　　　Their heads are green, and their hands are blue,
　　　　　　　　And they went to sea in a Sieve.

They sailed away in a Sieve, they did,
    In a Sieve they sailed so fast,
With only a beautiful pea-green veil
Tied with a riband by way of a sail,
    To a small tobacco-pipe mast;
And every one said, who saw them go,
'O won't they be soon upset, you know!
For the sky is dark, and the voyage is long;
And happen what may, it's extremely wrong
    In a Sieve to sail so fast!'
      Far and few, far and few,
        Are the lands where the Jumblies live;
        Their heads are green, and their hands are blue,
        And they went to sea in a Sieve.

The water it soon came in, it did,
    The water it soon came in;
So to keep them dry, they wrapped their feet
In a pinky paper all folded neat,
    And they fastened it down with a pin.
And they passed the night in a crockery-jar,
And each of them said, 'How wise we are!
Though the sky be dark, and the voyage be long,
Yet we never can think we were rash or wrong;
    While round in our Sieve we spin!'
      Far and few, far and few,
        Are the lands where the Jumblies live;
        Their heads are green, and their hands are blue,
        And they went to sea in a Sieve.

And all night long they sailed away;
    And when the sun went down,
They whistled and warbled a moony song
To the echoing sound of a coppery gong;
    In the shade of the mountains brown.
'O Timballo! How happy we are,
When we live in a sieve and a crockery-jar.
And all night long in the moonlight pale,
We sail away with a pea-green sail,
    In the shade of the mountains brown!'
        Far and few, far and few,
           Are the lands where the Jumblies live;
        Their heads are green, and their hands are blue,
           And they went to sea in a Sieve.

They sailed to the Western Sea, they did,
    To a land all covered with trees,
And they bought an Owl, and a useful Cart,
And a pound of Rice, and a Cranberry Tart,
    And a hive of silvery Bees.
And they bought a Pig, and some green Jackdaws,
And a lovely Monkey with lollipop paws,
And forty bottles of Ring-Bo-Ree,
    And no end of Stilton Cheese.
        Far and few, far and few,
           Are the lands where the Jumblies live;
        Their heads are green, and their hands are blue,
           And they went to sea in a Sieve.

And in twenty years they all came back,
   In twenty years or more,
And every one said, 'How tall they've grown!
For they've been to the Lakes, and the Terrible Zone,
   And the hills of the Chankly Bore';
And they drank their health, and gave them a feast
Of dumplings made of beautiful yeast;
And every one said, 'If we only live,
We too will go to sea in a Sieve,—
   To the hills of the Chankly Bore!'
     Far and few, far and few,
      Are the lands where the Jumblies live;
      Their heads are green, and their hands are blue,
      And they went to sea in a Sieve.

THE NUTCRACKERS AND THE SUGAR-TONGS

I

THE Nutcrackers sat by
 A plate on the table,
The Sugar-tongs sat by
 A plate at his side;
And the Nutcrackers said,
 'Don't you wish we were able
Along the blue hills and
 Green meadows to ride?
Must we drag on this stupid
 Existence for ever,
So idle and weary
 So full of remorse,—
While every one else takes
 His pleasure and never
Seems happy unless
 He is riding a horse?'

II

'Don't you think we could ride
    Without being instructed?
Without any saddle, or bridle, or spur?
    Our legs are so long,
And so aptly constructed,
    I'm sure that an accident
Could not occur.
Let us all of a sudden hop
    Down from the table,
And hustle downstairs,
    And each jump on a horse!
Shall we try? Shall we go?
    Do you think we are able?'
The Sugar-tongs answered distinctly,
    'Of course!'

III

So down the long staircase
    They hopped in a minute,
The Sugar-tongs snapped,
    And the Crackers said 'crack!'
The stable was open,
    The horses were in it;
Each took out a pony,
    And jumped on his back.
The Cat in a fright
    Scrambled out of the doorway,
The Mice tumbled out of
    A bundle of hay,
The brown and white Rats,
    And the black ones from Norway,
Screamed out, 'They are taking
    The horses away!'

IV

The whole of the household
    Was filled with amazement,
The Cups and the Saucers
    Danced madly about,
The Plates and the Dishes
    Looked out of the casement,
The Saltcellar stood on his
    Head with a shout,
The Spoons with a clatter
    Looked out of the lattice,
The Mustard-pot climbed
    Up the Gooseberry Pies,
The Soup-ladle peeped
    Through a heap of Veal Patties,
And squeaked with a ladle-like
    Scream of surprise.

V

The Frying-pan said,
    'It's an awful delusion!'
The Tea-kettle hissed
    And grew black in the face;
And they all rushed downstairs
    In the wildest confusion,
To see the great Nutcracker-
    Sugar-tong race.
And out of the stable,
    With screamings and laughter,
(Their ponies were cream-coloured,
    Speckled with brown),
The Nutcrackers first,
    And the Sugar-tongs after,
Rode all round the yard,
    And then all round the town.

VI

They rode through the street,
    And they rode by the station,
They galloped away
    To the beautiful shore;
In silence they rode,
    And 'made no observation,'
Save this : 'We will never
    Go back any more!'
And still you might hear,
    Till they rode out of hearing,
The Sugar-tongs snap,
    And the Crackers say 'crack!'
Till far in the distance,
    Their forms disappearing,
They faded away —
    And they never came back!

CALICO PIE

CALICO Pie,
The Little Birds fly
Down to the calico tree,
Their wings were blue,
And they sang 'Tilly-loo!'
Till away they flew,—
And they never came back to me!
They never came back!
They never came back!
They never came back to me!

Calico Jam,
The little Fish swam
Over the syllabub sea,
He took off his hat,
To the Sole and the Sprat,
And the Willeby-wat,—

But he never came back to me!
  He never came back!
  He never came back!
He never came back to me!

  Calico Ban,
  The little Mice ran,
To be ready in time for tea,
  Flippity flup,
  They drank it all up,
  And danced in the cup,—
But they never came back to me!
  They never came back!
  They never came back!
They never came back to me!

Calico Drum,
The Grasshoppers come,
The Butterfly, Beetle, and Bee,
Over the ground,
Around and round,
With a hop and a bound,—
But they never came back!
They never came back!
They never came back!
They never came back to me!

THE DONG WITH A LUMINOUS NOSE

WHEN awful darkness and silence reign
Over the great Gromboolian plain,
   Through the long, long wintry nights;—
When the angry breakers roar
As they beat on the rocky shore;—
    When Storm-clouds brood on the towering
       heights
Of the Hills of the Chankly Bore:—

Then, through the vast and gloomy dark,
There moves what seems a fiery spark,
   A lonely spark with silvery rays
   Piercing the coal-black night,—
   A meteor strange and bright:—
Hither and thither the vision strays,
   A single lurid light.

Slowly it wanders,—pauses,—creeps,—
Anon it sparkles,—flashes and leaps;
And ever as onward it gleaming goes
A light on the Bong-tree stems it throws.

And those who watch at that midnight hour
From Hall or Terrace, or lofty Tower,
Cry, as the wild light passes along,—
    'The Dong!—the Dong!
  The wandering Dong through the forest goes!
    The Dong! the Dong!
The Dong with a luminous Nose!'

    Long years ago
    The Dong was happy and gay,
Till he fell in love with a Jumbly Girl
  Who came to those shores one day.
For the Jumblies came in a Sieve, they did,—
Landing at eve near the Zemmery Fidd
    Where the Oblong Oysters grow,
  And the rocks are smooth and gray.
And all the woods and the valleys rang
With the Chorus they daily and nightly sang,—
    Far and few, far and few,
    Are the lands where the Jumblies live;
    Their heads are green, and their hands are blue,
    And they went to sea in a Sieve.'

Happily, happily passed those days!
    While the cheerful Jumblies staid;
  They danced in circlets all night long,
  To the plaintive pipe of the lively Dong,
    In moonlight, shine, or shade.
For day and night he was always there
By the side of the Jumbly Girl so fair,
With her sky-blue hands, and her sea-green hair,
Till the morning came of that hateful day
When the Jumblies sailed in their Sieve away,
And the Dong was left on the cruel shore
Gazing—gazing for evermore,—

31

Ever keeping his weary eyes on
That pea-green sail on the far horizon,—
Singing the Jumbly Chorus still
As he sat all day on the grassy hill,—
    'Far and few, far and few,
    Are the lands where the Jumblies live;
    Their heads are green, and their hands are blue,
    And they went to sea in a Sieve.'

But when the sun was low in the West;
    The Dong arose and said,—
  'What little sense I once possessed
  Has quite gone out of my head!'
And since that day he wanders still
By lake and forest, marsh and hill,
Singing—'O somewhere, in valley or plain
Might I find my Jumbly Girl again!
For ever I'll seek by lake and shore
Till I find my Jumbly Girl once more!'

  Playing a pipe with silvery squeaks,
  Since then his Jumbly Girl he seeks,
  And because by night he could not see,
  He gathered the bark of the Twangum Tree
    On the flowery plain that grows.
    And he wove him a wondrous Nose,—
  A Nose as strange as a Nose could be!
Of vast proportions and painted red,
And tied with cords to the back of his head.
  —In a hollow rounded space it ended
  With a luminous lamp within suspended
    All fenced about
    With a bandage stout
    To prevent the wind from blowing it out;—
  And with holes all round to send the light,
  In gleaming rays on the dismal night.

And now each night, and all night long,
Over those plains still roams the Dong;
And above the wail of the Chimp and Snipe
You may hear the squeak of his plaintive pipe
While ever he seeks, but seeks in vain
To meet with his Jumbly Girl again;
Lonely and wild—all night he goes,—
The Dong with a luminous Nose!
And all who watch at the midnight hour,
From Hall or Terrace, or lofty Tower,
Cry, as they trace the Meteor bright,
Moving along through the dreary night,—
    'This is the hour when forth he goes,
    The Dong with a luminous Nose!
    Yonder—over the plain he goes;
      He goes!
      He goes;
    The Dong with a luminous Nose!'

THE PELICAN CHORUS

KING and Queen of the Pelicans we;
No other Birds so grand we see!
None but we have feet like fins!
With lovely leathery throats and chins!
    Ploffskin, Pluffskin, Pelican jee!
     We think no Birds so happy as we!
    Plumpskin, Ploshkin, Pelican jill!
     We think so then, and we thought so still!

We live on the Nile. The Nile we love.
By night we sleep on the cliffs above.
By day we fish, and at eve we stand
On long bare islands of yellow sand.
And when the sun sinks slowly down
And the great rock walls grow dark and brown,
Where the purple river rolls fast and dim
And the ivory Ibis starlike skim,
Wing to wing we dance around,—
Stamping our feet with a flumpy sound,—
Opening our mouths as Pelicans ought,
And this is the song we nightly snort:

Ploffskin, Pluffskin, Pelican jee!
We think no Birds so happy as we!
Plumpskin, Ploshkin, Pelican jill!
We think so then, and we thought so still!

Last year came out our Daughter, Dell;
And all the Birds received her well.
To do her honour, a feast we made
For every Bird that can swim or wade.
Herons and Gulls, and Cormorants black,
Cranes, and Flamingoes with scarlet back,
Plovers and Storks, and Geese in clouds,
Swans and Dilberry Ducks in crowds.
Thousands of Birds in wondrous flight!
They ate and drank and danced all night,
And echoing back from the rocks you heard
Multitude-echoes from Bird and Bird,—
Ploffskin, Pluffskin, Pelican jee!
We think no Birds so happy as we!
Plumpskin, Ploshkin, Pelican jill!
We think so then, and we thought so still!

Yes, they came; and among the rest,
The King of the Cranes all grandly dressed.
Such a lovely tail! Its feathers float
Between the ends of his blue dress-coat;
With pea-green trowsers all so neat,
And a delicate frill to hide his feet,—
(For though no one speaks of it, every one knows,
He has got no webs between his toes!)

As soon as he saw our Daughter Dell,
In violent love that Crane King fell,—
On seeing her waddling form so fair,
With a wreath of shrimps in her short white hair,
And before the end of the next long day,

Our Dell had given her heart away;
For the King of the Cranes had won that heart,
With a Crocodile's egg and a large fish-tart.
She vowed to marry the King of the Cranes,
Leaving the Nile for stranger plains;
And away they flew in a gathering crowd
Of endless Birds in a lengthening cloud.
      Ploffskin, Pluffskin, Pelican jee!
      We think no Birds so happy as we!
      Plumpskin, Ploshkin, Pelican jill!
      We think so then, and we thought so still!

And far away in the twilight sky,
We heard them singing a lessening cry,—
Farther and farther till out of sight,
And we stood alone in the silent night!
Often since, in the nights of June,
We sit on the sand and watch the moon;—
She has gone to the great Gromboolian plain,
And we probably never shall meet again!
Oft, in the long still nights of June,
We sit on the rocks and watch the moon;—
—She dwells by the streams of the Chankly Bore,
And we probably never shall see her more.
      Ploffskin, Pluffskin, Pelican jee!
      We think no Birds so happy as we!
      Plumpskin, Ploshkin, Pelican jill!
      We think so then, and we thought so still!

THE COURTSHIP
OF THE YONGHY-BONGHY-BO

ON the Coast of Coromandel
    Where the early pumpkins blow,
  In the middle of the woods
  Lived the Yonghy-Bonghy-Bò.
Two old chairs, and half a candle,—
One old jug without a handle,—
    These were all his worldly goods:
    In the middle of the woods,
    These were all the worldly goods,
  Of the Yonghy-Bonghy-Bò,
  Of the Yonghy-Bonghy-Bò.

Once, among the Bong-trees walking
    Where the early pumpkins blow,
       To a little heap of stones
    Came the Yonghy-Bonghy-Bò.
There he heard a Lady talking,
To some milk-white Hens of Dorking,—
      ''Tis the Lady Jingly Jones!
      On that little heap of stones
      Sits the Lady Jingly Jones!'
    Said the Yonghy-Bonghy-Bò,
    Said the Yonghy-Bonghy-Bò.

'Lady Jingly! Lady Jingly!
    Sitting where the pumpkins blow,
       Will you come and be my wife?'
    Said the Yonghy-Bonghy-Bò.
'I am tired of living singly,—
On this coast so wild and shingly,'—
      I'm a-weary of my life;
      If you'll come and be my wife,
      Quite serene would be my life!'—
    Said the Yonghy-Bonghy-Bò
    Said the Yonghy-Bonghy-Bò.

'On this Coast of Coromandel,
    Shrimps and watercresses grow,
       Prawns are plentiful and cheap,'
    Said the Yonghy-Bonghy-Bò.
'You shall have my chairs and candle,
And my jug without a handle!—
      Gaze upon the rolling deep
      (Fish is plentiful and cheap);
      As the sea, my love is deep!'
    Said the Yonghy-Bonghy-Bò,
    Said the Yonghy-Bonghy-Bò.

Lady Jingly answered sadly,
    And her tears began to flow,—
        'Your proposal comes too late,
    Mr Yonghy-Bonghy-Bò!
I would be your wife most gladly!'
(Here she twirled her fingers madly)
        'But in England I've a mate!
        Yes! you've asked me far too late,
        For in England I've a mate,
    Mr Yonghy-Bonghy-Bò!
    Mr Yonghy-Bonghy-Bò!

'Mr Jones—(his name is Handel,—
    Handel Jones, Esquire, & Co.)
        Dorking fowls delights to send,
    Mr Yonghy-Bonghy-Bò!
Keep, oh! keep your chairs and candle,
And your jug without a handle,—
        I can merely be your friend!
        —Should my Jones more Dorkings send,
        I will give you three, my friend!
    Mr Yonghy-Bonghy-Bò!
    Mr Yonghy-Bonghy-Bò!

'Though you've such a tiny body,
    And your head so large doth grow,—
        Though your hat may blow away,
    Mr Yonghy-Bonghy-Bò!
Though you're such a Hoddy Doddy—
Yet I wish that I could modi-
        fy the words I needs must say!
        Will you please to go away?
        That is all I have to say—
    Mr Yonghy-Bonghy-Bò!
    Mr Yonghy-Bonghy-Bò!'

Down the slippery slopes of Myrtle,
    Where the early pumpkins blow,
        To the calm and silent sea
        Fled the Yonghy-Bonghy-Bò.
There, beyond the Bay of Gurtle,
Lay a large and lively Turtle;—
        'You're the Cove,' he said, 'for me;
        On your back beyond the sea,
        Turtle, you shall carry me!'
    Said the Yonghy-Bonghy-Bo,
    Said the Yonghy-Bonghy-Bo.

Through the silent-roaring ocean
    Did the Turtle swiftly go;
        Holding fast upon his shell
    Rode the Yonghy-Bonghy-Bò.
With a sad primreval motion
Towards the sunset isles of Boshen
        Still the Turtle bore him well.
        Holding fast upon his shell,
          'Lady Jingly Jones, farewell!'
    Sang the Yonghy-Bonghy-Bò,
    Sang the Yonghy-Bonghy-Bò.

From the Coast of Coromandel,
    Did that Lady never go;
        On that heap of stones she mourns
    For the Yonghy-Bonghy-Bò.
On that Coast of Coromandel,
In his jug without a handle,
        Still she weeps, and daily moans;
        On that little heap of stones
        To her Dorking Hens she moans,
    For the Yonghy-Bonghy-Bò,
    For the Yonghy-Bonghy-Bò.

THE POBBLE WHO HAS NO TOES

THE Pobble who has no toes
   Had once as many as we;
When they said, 'Some day you may lose
     them all';—
   He replied,—'Fish fiddle de-dee!'
And his Aunt Jobiska made him drink,
Lavender water tinged with pink,
For she said, 'The World in general knows
There's nothing so good for a Pobble's toes!'

The Pobble who has no toes,
   Swam across the Bristol Channel;
But before he set out he wrapped his nose
   In a piece of scarlet flannel.
For his Aunt Jobiska said, 'No harm
Can come to his toes if his nose is warm;
And it's perfectly known that a Pobble's toes
Are safe,—provided he minds his nose.'

The Pobble swam fast and well,
    And when boats or ships came near him
He tinkledy-binkledy-winkled a bell,
    So that all the world could hear him.
And all the Sailors and Admirals cried,
When they saw him nearing the further side,—
'He has gone to fish, for his Aunt Jobiska's
Runcible Cat with crimson whiskers!'

But before he touched the shore,
    The shore of the Bristol Channel,
A sea-green Porpoise carried away
    His wrapper of scarlet flannel.
And when he came to observe his feet,
Formerly garnished with toes so neat,
His face at once became forlorn
On perceiving that all his toes were gone!

And nobody ever knew
    From that dark day to the present,
Whoso had taken the Pobble's toes,
    In a manner so far from pleasant.
Whether the shrimps or crawfish gray,
Or crafty Mermaids stole them away—
Nobody knew; and nobody knows
How the Pobble was robbed of his twice five toes!

The Pobble who has no toes
    Was placed in a friendly Bark,
And they rowed him back, and carried him up,
    To his Aunt Jobiska's Park.
And she made him a feast at his earnest wish
Of eggs and buttercups fried with fish;—
And she said,—'It's a fact the whole world knows,
That Pobbles are happier without their toes.'

MR AND MRS DISCOBBOLOS
FIRST PART

MR AND MRS DISCOBBOLOS
    Climbed to the top of a wall,
  And they sat to watch the sunset sky
  And to hear the Nupiter Piffkin cry
    And the Biscuit Buffalo call.
They took up a roll and some Camomile tea,
And both were as happy as happy could be—
    Till Mrs Discobbolos said,—
    'Oh! W! X! Y! Z!
    It has just come into my head—
Suppose we should happen to fall!!!!!
    Darling Mr Discobbolos?

  ,

'Suppose we should fall down flumpetty
    Just like two pieces of stone!
  On to the thorns,—or into the moat!
  What would become of your new green coat?
    And might you not break a bone?
It never occurred to me before—
That perhaps we shall never go down any more!'
    And Mrs Discobbolos said-
    'Oh! W! X! Y! Z!
    What put it into your head
To climb up this wall?—my own
    Darling Mr Discobbolos?'

Mr Discobbolos answered,—
    'At first it gave me pain,—
   And I felt my ears turn perfectly pink
   When your exclamation made me think
    We might never get down again!
But now I believe it is wiser far
To remain for ever just where we are.'—
    And Mr Discobbolos said,
    'Oh! W! X! Y! Z!
    It has just come into my head'—
  —We shall never go down again—
    Dearest Mrs Discobbolos!'

So Mr and Mrs Discobbolos
    Stood up, and began to sing,
   'Far away from hurry and strife
   Here we will pass the rest of life,
    Ding a dong, ding dong, ding!
We want no knives nor forks nor chairs,
No tables nor carpets nor household cares,
    From worry of life we've fled—
    Oh! W! X! Y! Z!
    There is no more trouble ahead
    Sorrow or any such thing—
    For Mr and Mrs Discobbolos!'

MR AND MRS DISCOBBOLOS
SECOND PART

MR AND MRS DISCOBBOLOS
    Lived on the top of the wall,
   For twenty years, a month and a day,
   Till their hair had grown all pearly gray,
    And their teeth began to fall.
They never were ill, or at all dejected,
By all admired, and by some respected,
    Till Mrs Discobbolos said,
    'Oh! W! X! Y! Z!
    It has just come into my head,
   We have no more room at all—
       Darling Mr Discobbolos!

'Look at our six fine boys!
    And our six sweet girls so fair!
   Upon this wall they have all been born,
   And not one of the twelve has happened to fall
    Through my maternal care!
Surely they should not pass their lives
Without any chance of husbands or wives!'
And Mrs Discobbolos said,
     'Oh! W! X! Y! Z!
     Did it never come into your head
     That our lives must be lived elsewhere,
     Dearest Mr Discobbolos?

'They have never been at a ball,
    Nor have even seen a bazaar!
   Nor have heard folks say in a tone all hearty,
   "What loves of girls" (at a garden party)
    "Those Misses Discobbolos are!"

Morning and night it drives me wild
To think of the fate of each darling child!'
        But Mr Discobbolos said,
        'Oh! W! X! Y! Z!
        What has come to your fiddledum head!
    What a runcible goose you are!
            Octopod Mrs Discobbolos!'

Suddenly Mr Discobbolos
        Slid from the top of the wall;
    And beneath it he dug a dreadful trench,
    And filled it with dynamite, gunpowder gench,
        And aloud he began to call—
'Let the wild bee sing,
And the blue bird hum!
For the end of your lives has certainly come!'
        And Mrs Discobbolos said,
        'Oh! W! X! Y! Z!
        We shall presently all be dead,
    On this ancient runcible wall,
            Terrible Mr Discobbolos!'

Pensively, Mr Discobbolos
        Sat with his back to the wall;
    He lighted a match, and fired the train,
    And the mortified mountain echoed again
        To the sound of an awful fall!
And all the Discobbolos family flew
In thousands of bits to the sky so blue,
        And no one was left to have said,
        'Oh! W! X! Y! Z!
        Has it come into anyone's head
    That the end has happened to all
            Of the whole of the Clan Discobbolos?'

THE QUANGLE WANGLE'S HAT

ON the top of the Crumpetty Tree
   The Quangle Wangle sat,
But his face you could not see,
   On account of his Beaver Hat.
For his Hat was a hundred and two feet wide,
With ribbons and bibbons on every side
And bells, and buttons, and loops, and lace,
So that nobody ever could see the face
     Of the Quangle Wangle Quee.

The Quangle Wangle said
   To himself on the Crumpetty Tree,—
'Jam; and jelly; and bread;
   Are the best of food for me!
But the longer I live on this Crumpetty Tree,
The plainer than ever it seems to me
That very few people come this way,
And that life on the whole is far from gay!'
     Said the Quangle Wangle Quee.

But there came to the Crumpetty Tree,
    Mr and Mrs Canary;
And they said,—'Did ever you see
    Any spot so charmingly airy?
May we build a nest on your lovely Hat?
Mr Quangle Wangle, grant us that!
O please let us come and build a nest
Of whatever material suits you best,
        Mr Quangle Wangle Queel'

And besides, to the Crumpetty Tree
    Came the Stork, the Duck, and the Owl;
The Snail and the Bumble-Bee,
    The Frog, and the Fimble Fowl;
(The Fimble Fowl, with a Corkscrew leg);
And all of them said,—'We humbly beg,
We may build our homes on your lovely Hat,—
Mr Quangle Wangle, grant us that!
        Mr Quangle Wangle Quee!'

And the Golden Grouse came there,
    And the Pobble who has no toes,—
And the small Olympian bear,—
    And the Dong with a luminous nose.
And the Blue Baboon, who played the flute,—
And the Orient Calf from the Land of Tute,—
And the Attery Squash, and the Bisky Bat,—
All came and built on the lovely Hat
        Of the Quangle Wangle Quee.

And the Quangle Wangle said
   To himself on the Crumpetty Tree,—
'When all these creatures move
   What a wonderful noise there'll be!'
And at night by the light of the Mulberry moon
They danced to the Flute of the Blue Baboon,
On the broad green leaves of the Crumpetty Tree,
And all were as happy as happy could be,
     With the Quangle Wangle Quee.

THE CUMMERBUND
AN INDIAN POEM

SHE sat upon her Dobie,[1]
　To watch the Evening Star,
And all the Punkahs[2] as they passed
　Cried, 'My! how fair you are!'
Around her bower, with quivering leaves,
　The tall Kamsamahs[3] grew,
And Kitmutgars[4] in wild festoons
　Hung down from Tchokis[5] blue.

Below her home the river rolled
　With soft meloobious sound,
Where golden-finned Chuprassies[6] swam,
　In myriads circling round.
Above, on tallest trees remote,
　Green Ayahs perched alone,
And all night long the Mussak[7] moan'd
　Its melancholy tone.

And where the purple Nullahs[8] threw
　Their branches far and wide,—
And silvery Goreewallahs[9] flew
　In silence, side by side,—

———————

1 Washerman
2 Fan
3 Butler
4 Waiter at Table
5 Police or post station
6 Office messenger
7 Water skin
8 Watercourse
9 Groom

The little Bheesties'[1] twittering cry
    Rose on the fragrant air,
And oft the angry Jampan[2] howled
    Deep in his hateful lair.

She sat upon her Dobie,—
    She heard the Nimmak[3] hum,
When all at once a cry arose:
    'The Cummerbund[4] is come!'
In vain she fled;—with open jaws
    The angry monster followed,
And so, (before assistance came),
    That Lady Fair was swollowed.

They sought in vain for even a bone
    Respectfully to bury,—
They said, 'Hers was a dreadful fate!'
    (And Echo answered 'Very.')
They nailed her Dobie to the wall,
    Where last her form was seen,
And underneath they wrote these words,
    In yellow, blue, and green:—

Beware, ye Fair! Ye Fair, beware!
    Nor sit out late at night,—
Lest horrid Cummerbunds should come,
    And swollow you outright.

1 Water-carrier
2 Sedan chair
3 Salt
4 Waist-sash

THE AKOND OF SWAT

WHO or why, or which, or *what*,
Is the Akond of SWAT?

Is he tall or short, or dark or fair?
Does he sit on a stool or a sofa or chair,
            or SQUAT,
        The Akond of Swat?

Is he wise or foolish, young or old?
Does he drink his soup and his coffee cold,
            or HOT,
        The Akond of Swat?

Does he sing or whistle, jabber or talk,
And when riding abroad does he gallop or walk,
            or TROT,
        The Akond of Swat?

Does he wear a turban, a fez, or a hat?
Does he sleep on a mattress, a bed, or a mat,
            or a COT,
        The Akond of Swat?

When he writes a copy in round-hand size,
Does he cross his T's and finish his I's
            with a DOT,
        The Akond of Swat?

Can he write a letter concisely clear
Without a speck or a smudge or smear
            or BLOT,
        The Akond of Swat?

Do his people like him extremely well?
Or do they, whenever they can, rebel,
      or PLOT,
    At the Akond of Swat?

If he catches them then, either old or young,
Does he have them chopped in pieces or hung,
      or SHOT,
    The Akond of Swat?

Do his people prig in the lanes or park?
Or even at times, when days are dark,
      GAROTTE?
    O the Akond of Swat!

Does he study the wants of his own dominion?
Or doesn't he care for public opinion
      a JOT,
    The Akond of Swat?

To amuse his mind do his people show him
Pictures, or any one's last new poem,
      or WHAT,
    For the Akond of Swat?

At night if he suddenly screams and wakes,
Do they bring him only a few small cakes,
      or a LOT,
    For the Akond of Swat?

Does he live on turnips, tea, or tripe?
Does he like his shawl to be marked with a stripe,
      or a DOT,
    The Akond of Swat?

Does he like to lie on his back in a boat
Like the lady who lived in that isle remote,
       SHALLOTT,
    The Akond of Swat?

Is he quiet, or always making a fuss?
Is his steward a Swiss or a Swede or a Russ,
      or a SCOT,
    The Akond of Swat?

Does he like to sit by the calm blue wave?
Or to sleep and snore in a dark green cave,
      or a GROTT,
    The Akond of Swat?

Does he drink small beer from a silver jug?
Or a bowl? or a glass? or a cup? or a mug?
      or a POT,
    The Akond of Swat?

Does he beat his wife with a gold-topped pipe,
When she lets the gooseberries grow too ripe,
      or ROT,
    The Akond of Swat?

Does he wear a white tie when he dines with friends,
And tie it neat in a bow with ends,
      or a KNOT,
    The Akond of Swat?

Does he like new cream, and hate mince-pies?
When he looks at the sun does he wink his eyes,
      or NOT,
    The Akond of Swat?

Does he teach his subjects to roast and bake?
Does he sail about on an inland lake,
    in a YACHT,
      The Akond of Swat?

Some one, or nobody, knows, I wot,
Who or which or why or what
      Is the Akond of Swat!

NOTE—For the existence of this potentate see Indian newspapers, *passim*. The proper way to read the verses is to make an immense emphasis on the monosyllabic rhymes, which indeed ought to be shouted out by a chorus.

INCIDENTS IN THE LIFE OF MY
UNCLE ARLY

O MY agèd Uncle Arly!
Sitting on a heap of Barley
   Thro' the silent hours of night,—
Close beside a leafy thicket:—
On his nose there was a Cricket,—
In his hat a Railway-Ticket;—
   (But his shoes were far too tight).

Long ago, in youth, he squander'd
All his goods away, and wander'd
   To the Tiniskoop-hills afar.
There on golden sunsets blazing,
Every evening found him gazing,—
Singing,—'Orb! you're quite amazing!
   How I wonder what you are!'

Like the ancient Medes and Persians,
Always by his own exertions
   He subsisted on those hills;—
Whiles,—by teaching children spelling,—
Or at times by merely yelling,—
Or at intervals by selling
   'Propter's Nicodemus Pills.'

Later, in his morning rambles
He perceived the moving brambles
   Something square and white disclose;—
'Twas a First-class Railway-Ticket;
But, on stooping down to pick it
Off the ground,—a pea-green Cricket
   Settled on my uncle's Nose.

Never—never more,—oh! never,
Did that Cricket leave him ever,—
    Dawn or evening, day or night;—
Clinging as a constant treasure,—
Chirping with a cheerious measure,—
Wholly to my uncle's pleasure,—
    (Though his shoes were far too tight).

So for three-and-forty winters,
Till his shoes were worn to splinters,
    All those hills he wander'd o'er,—
Sometimes silent;—sometimes yelling;—
Till he came to Bodey-Melling,
Near his old ancestral dwelling;—
    (But his shoes were far too tight).

On a little heap of Barley
Died my aged uncle Arly,
    And they buried him one night;—
Close beside the leafy thicket;—
There,—his hat and Railway-Ticket;—
There,—his ever-faithful Cricket;—
    (But his shoes were far too tight).

SELECTED LIMERICKS

AN OLD MAN WITH A BEARD

There was an Old Man with a beard,
Who said, "It is just as I feared!—
    Two Owls and a Hen,
    four Larks and a Wren,
Have all built their nests in my beard.

AN OLD PERSON OF HURST

There was an Old Person of Hurst,
Who drank when he was not athirst;
    When they said, "You'll grow fatter,"
    He answered, "What matter?"
That globular Person of Hurst.

A YOUNG PERSON OF SMYRNA

There was a Young Person of Smyrna,
Whose Grandmother threatened to burn her;
    But she seized on the cat,
    And said, 'Granny, burn that!
You incongruous Old Woman of Smyrna!'

A YOUNG LADY WHOSE BONNET

There was a Young Lady whose bonnet,
Came untied when the birds sat upon it;
    But she said: 'I don't care!
    All the birds in the air
Are welcome to sit on my bonnet!'

A YOUNG LADY OF HULL

There was a Young Lady of Hull,
Who was chased by a virulent bull;
    But she seized on a spade,
    And called out, 'Who's afraid?'
Which distracted that virulent bull.

AN OLD MAN OF WHITEHAVEN

There was an Old Man of Whitehaven,
Who danced a quadrille with a Raven;
    But they said, "It's absurd
    to encourage this bird!"
So they smashed that Old Man of Whitehaven.

A YOUNG LADY OF TYRE

There was a Young Lady of Tyre,
Who swept the loud chords of a lyre;
    At the sound of each sweep
    she enraptured the deep,
And enchanted the city of Tyre.

AN OLD MAN OF MARSEILLES

There was an Old Man of Marseilles,
Whose daughters wore bottle-green veils;
    They caught several Fish,
    Which they put in a dish,
And sent to their Pa' at Marseilles.

AN OLD PERSON OF BASING

There was an Old Person of Basing,
Whose presence of mind was amazing;
    He purchased a steed,
    Which he rode at full speed,
And escaped from the people of Basing.

A YOUNG LADY OF BUTE

The was a Young Lady of Bute,
Who played on a silver-gilt flute;
    She played several jigs,
    To her uncle's white pigs,
That amusing Young Lady of Bute.

AN OLD PERSON OF CROMER

There was an Old Person of Cromer,
Who stood on one leg to read Homer;
  When he found he grew stiff,
  He jumped over the cliff,
Which concluded that Person of Cromer.

AN OLD MAN OF BOHEMIA

There was an Old Man of Bohemia,
Whose daughter was christened Euphemia;
  But one day, to his grief,
  She married a thief,
Which grieved that Old Man of Bohemia.